My Bible counting book

3

2

1

Anne Pilmoor

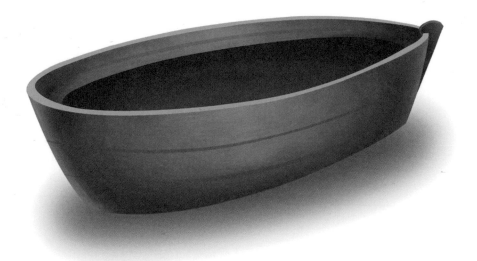

1 one

One boat

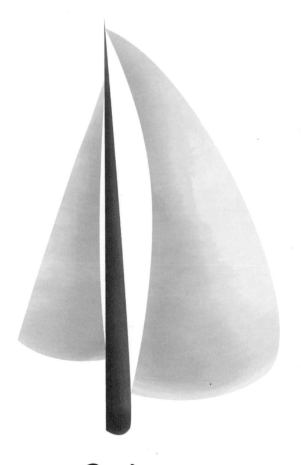

2 two

Two large sails

3 three

Three portholes

4 four

Four fishermen

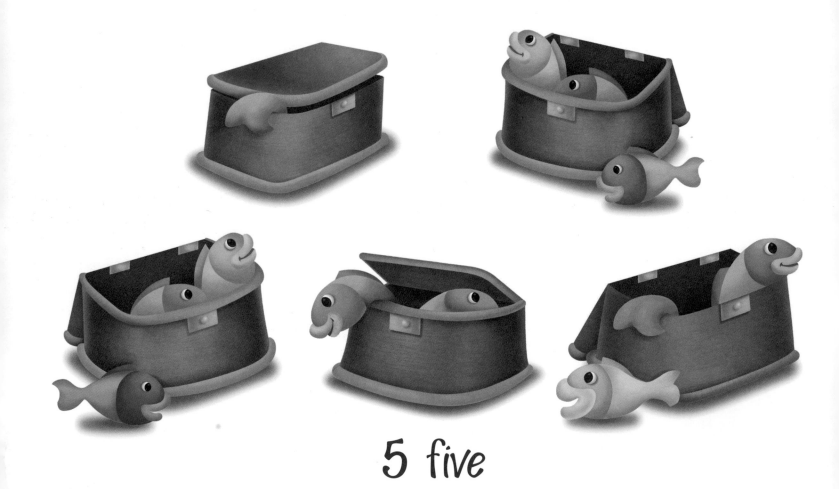

5 five

Five fishing baskets

6 six

Six crawling crabs

7 seven

Seven pretty shells

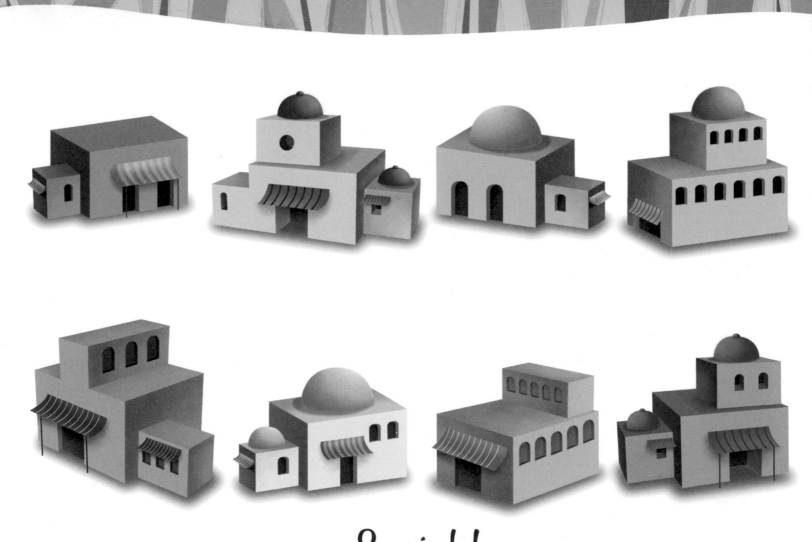

8 eight

Eight
houses on the hillside

9 nine

Nine twinkling stars

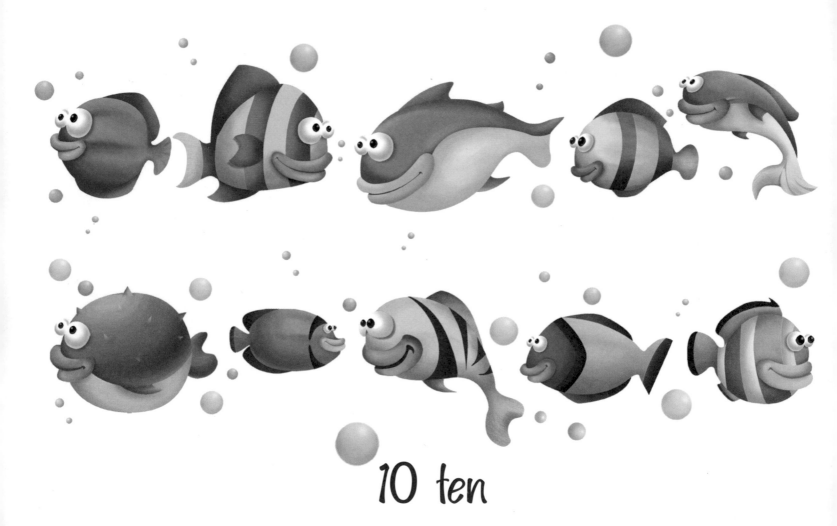

10 ten

Ten fish
caught in the net

Jesus said:
'I will make you fishers of men.'
And now I can count from one to ten!

First published in 2010

Copyright © 2010 Autumn House Publishing (Europe) Ltd

British Library Cataloguing in Publication Data.

A catalogue record for this book is available from the British Library.

ISBN 978-1-906381-89-9

Published by Autumn House (Europe), Grantham, Lincolnshire.

Illustrated by Chiari Vercesi.

Printed in Thailand.